D0984658

SPORTS GREAT DIKEMBE MUTOMBO

—Sports Great Books—

BASEBALL

Sports Great Jim Abbott
0-89490-395-0/ Savage

Sports Great Bobby Bonilla
0-89490-417-5/ Knapp

Sports Great Ken Griffey, Jr.
0-7660-1266-2/ Savage

Sports Great Orel Hershiser
0-89490-389-6/ Knapp

Sports Great Bo Jackson
0-89490-281-4/ Knapp

Sports Great Greg Maddux
0-89490-873-1/ Thornley

Sports Great Kirby Puckett
0-89490-392-6/ Aaseng

Sports Great Cal Ripken, Jr.
0-89490-387-X/ Macnow

Sports Great Nolan Ryan
0-89490-394-2/ Lace

Sports Great Darryl Strawberry
0-89490-291-1/ Torres & Sullivan

Sports Great Frank Thomas
0-7660-1269-7/ Deane

BASKETBALL

**Sports Great Charles Barkley
(Revised Edition)**
0-7660-1004-X/ Macnow

Sports Great Larry Bird
0-89490-368-3/ Kavanagh

Sports Great Kobe Bryant
0-7660-1264-6/ Macnow

Sports Great Muggsy Bogues
0-89490-876-6/ Rekela

Sports Great Patrick Ewing
0-89490-369-1/ Kavanagh

Sports Great Kevin Garnett
0-7660-1263-8/ Macnow

Sports Great Anfernee Hardaway
0-89490-758-1/ Rekela

Sports Great Juwan Howard
0-7660-1065-1/ Savage

**Sports Great Magic Johnson
(Revised and Expanded)**
0-89490-348-9/ Haskins

**Sports Great Michael Jordan
(Revised Edition)**
0-89490-978-9/ Aaseng

Sports Great Jason Kidd
0-7660-1001-5/ Torres

Sports Great Karl Malone
0-89490-599-6/ Savage

Sports Great Reggie Miller
0-89490-874-X/ Thornley

Sports Great Alonzo Mourning
0-89490-875-8/ Fortunato

Sports Great Dikembe Mutombo
0-7660-1267-0/ Torres

**Sports Great Shaquille O'Neal
(Revised Edition)**
0-7660-1003-1/ Sullivan

Sports Great Scottie Pippen
0-89490-755-7/ Bjarkman

Sports Great Mitch Richmond
0-7660-1070-8/ Grody

**Sports Great David Robinson
(Revised Edition)**
0-7660-1077-5/ Aaseng

Sports Great Dennis Rodman
0-89490-759-X/ Thornley

Sports Great John Stockton
0-89490-598-8/ Aaseng

Sports Great Isiah Thomas
0-89490-374-8/ Knapp

Sports Great Chris Webber
0-7660-1069-4/ Macnow

Sports Great Dominique Wilkins
0-89490-754-9/ Bjarkman

FOOTBALL

Sports Great Troy Aikman
0-89490-593-7/ Macnow

Sports Great Jerome Bettis
0-89490-872-3/ Majewski

Sports Great John Elway
0-89490-282-2/ Fox

Sports Great Brett Favre
0-7660-1000-7/ Savage

Sports Great Jim Kelly
0-89490-670-4/ Harrington

Sports Great Joe Montana
0-89490-371-3/ Kavanagh

Sports Great Jerry Rice
0-89490-419-1/ Dickey

**Sports Great Barry Sanders
(Revised Edition)**
0-7660-1067-8/ Knapp

Sports Great Deion Sanders
0-7660-1068-6/ Macnow

Sports Great Emmitt Smith
0-7660-1002-3/ Grabowski

Sports Great Herschel Walker
0-89490-207-5/ Benagh

OTHER

Sports Great Michael Chang
0-7660-1223-9/ Ditchfield

Sports Great Oscar De La Hoya
0-7660-1066-X/ Torres

Sports Great Wayne Gretzky
0-89490-757-3/ Rappoport

Sports Great Mario Lemieux
0-89490-596-1/ Knapp

Sports Great Eric Lindros
0-89490-871-5/ Rappoport

Sports Great Steffi Graf
0-89490-597-X/ Knapp

Sports Great Pete Sampras
0-89490-756-5/ Sherrow

SPORTS GREAT DIKEMBE MUTOMBO

John Albert Torres

Enslow Publishers, Inc.

40 Industrial Road   PO Box 38
Box 398   Aldershot
Berkeley Heights, NJ 07922   Hants GU12 6BP
USA   UK
http://www.enslow.com

Library of Congress Cataloging-in-Publication Data

Torres, John Albert
    Sports great Dikembe Mutombo / John Albert Torres.
       p. cm. — (Sports great books)
    Includes index.
    Summary: A biography of Dikembe "Mount" Mutombo, who came to the United
States from Zaire to attend Georgetown University on an academic scholarship and
went on to become a basketball star with the Denver Nuggets and Atlanta Hawks.
    ISBN 0-7660-1267-0
    1. Mutombo, Dikembe Juvenile literature. 2. Basketball players—Congo
(Democratic Republic) Biography Juvenile literature. [1. Mutombo, Dikembe.
2. Basketball players.] I. Title. II. Title: Dikembe Mutombo. III. Series.
GV884.M886T67   2000
796.323'092—dc21
[B]   99-30160
                                                   CIP

Printed in the United States of America

10 9 8 7 6 5 4 3 2

To Our Readers: We have done our best to make sure all Internet Addresses in this book were
active and appropriate when we went to press. However, the author and the publisher have
no control over and assume no liability for the material available on those Internet sites or
on other Web sites they may link to. Any comments or suggestions can be sent by e-mail to
comments@enslow.com or to the address on the back cover.

Illustration Credits: Andrew D. Bernstein/NBA Photos, pp. 21, 35; NBA Photo
Library, p. 52; Phil McCollum/NBA Photos, p. 16; Rocky Widner/NBA Photos, p.
33; Scott Cunningham/NBA Photos, pp. 8, 10, 12, 19, 24, 28, 29, 40, 44, 46, 50, 54,
56; Thomas Turck/NBA Photos, p. 37.

Cover Illustration: Rocky Widner/NBA Photos.

Contents

Chapter 1

The series was supposed to be a huge mismatch. It was David against Goliath. It was the lowly Denver Nuggets, who had somehow snuck into the playoffs with a mediocre 42–40 record, against the powerhouse, the heavily favored Seattle SuperSonics. The Sonics had finished the 1993–94 season with a 63–19 mark, the best in the NBA. But little did the Seattle players know that they were about to face a David with a giant of their own. The giant was Denver's seven-foot two-inch center, Dikembe Mutombo.

The Seattle powerhouse jumped out to a 2–0 series lead against the lowly Nuggets and treated Denver as if it were just a stop along the way to an NBA championship. Then the giant player from Africa, Mutombo, had a dream. He dreamed that he could lead his team in combat against the Sonics. He dreamed that the Nuggets could sweep their rivals in three straight games.

Mutombo inspired the team. He took on a warrior-like mentality. He also decided that the slam-dunking Sonics

Dikembe Mutombo takes a shot over the outstretched arm of Ike Austin. At seven-feet two-inches tall, Mutombo is a formidable presence on the basketball court.

would no longer get an easy basket. Mutombo decided to try and block just about every shot in his vicinity.

"Their game was from the paint, from the inside," he said. "To me, going for blocks was the only way we could win."

Mutombo became ferocious. He blocked an NBA playoff-record 31 shots in a five-game series. He intimidated the Sonics away from the basket and made them take jump shots far from the paint. Seattle was not a good jump-shooting team, and they had a hard time scoring.

Even Seattle's coach, George Karl, recognized the effect that Mutombo had on the Sonics. "He got in our players' heads and never left," Karl said.

Denver rode great performances by Mutombo, Reggie Williams, Robert Pack, and Brian Williams to win Games 3 and 4. There was one game left, Game 5 in Seattle.

In one sequence, early in this final and deciding game, Mutombo set the tone for what looked to be an incredible upset. He leaped high in the air to block a fadeaway jump shot by Sam Perkins. Seattle point guard Gary Payton was able to corral the loose ball, and he tried shooting over Mutombo. Big mistake. Mutombo swatted the ball away, and the Nuggets recovered. From that point on, the Sonics knew it would be a tough game to win.

Somehow the Denver Nuggets had just enough to defeat their Goliath. As the final buzzer sounded, Mutombo was overwhelmed. He fell to the floor of the Seattle Center Coliseum and started to cry. He lay sprawled out on the floor, with his arms stretched out like wings, moved to joy and tears. His teammates ran over and hugged him. He had shown the NBA and its fans what a force he truly was. No eighth-seeded team had ever before defeated a first seed in the playoffs. The Denver Nuggets had made history, flying past the Sonics on the wings of a giant.

Mutombo celebrates a fine play. While he was with the Nuggets in 1994, the entire city of Denver celebrated the playoff victory over the Sonics.

Mutombo's performance, and his open display of emotion, stayed with reporters and fans alike. "The most indelible image of Dikembe Mutombo's NBA career will be his unbridled celebration while sprawled on the Seattle Coliseum court after Denver's historic playoff upset of the SuperSonics," wrote Seattle columnist Glenn Nelson.

The Nuggets then faced another heavily favored team, the Utah Jazz, in the Western Conference Semifinals. Utah was led by future Hall of Fame players Karl Malone and John Stockton. Many people counted the Nuggets out, but there was no quit in Mutombo and his teammates.

"There's nobody else in our league who has the intimidating presence he has in the hole," said veteran NBA coach Don Nelson. "He's one of a kind."

The Jazz seemed like too much for the Nuggets, as they easily won the first three games of the series. But once again, Denver rallied around their center, Dikembe Mutombo, who was now known as Mount Mutombo. The Nuggets won the next three games of the series, to force a deciding seventh game. But Karl Malone and John Stockton were too much for Mutombo and his Nuggets. The Jazz prevailed, 91–81, to eliminate the Nuggets and end their improbable playoff run.

Mutombo was simply dominating in the playoffs, especially on the defensive end. He averaged 13.3 points, 12.0 rebounds, and 5.75 blocks, though the Nuggets fell in seven tough games. In the seven games against Utah, Mutombo broke his own record for blocked shots in a series by blocking 38 of them.

But the playoffs accomplished something else. Now it seemed that the whole basketball world knew what sort of a player Dikembe Mutombo was. A giant with a warrior's heart, he would be one of the league's most dominating players for years to come.

During his third season of playing professional basketball, Mutombo became the NBA's premier shot-blocker.

His shot-blocking and intense rebounding came as no surprise to fans and players who had watched Mutombo play all year. In just his third season of professional basketball, he had become the NBA's premier shot-blocker. He led the league with 4.10 blocked shots per game. He was also a fierce rebounder, ranking sixth in the league, with 11.8 boards per game.

What was even more amazing was that, after only three seasons, Mutombo was already the Denver Nuggets' all-time leader in blocked shots. The pleasant Mutombo was also becoming a fan favorite. On November 26, 1993 he led the Nuggets to a victory over the Portland Trail Blazers. He thrilled the fans with an incredible performance. Mutombo recorded 17 points, 13 rebounds, and 11 blocked shots! It was truly a dominating performance.

Dikembe Mutombo had made a lot of progress. He had come a long way for someone who grew up in the faraway African country of Zaire [now the Democratic Republic of Congo], a place not known for basketball. He had been laughed at as a child because he was so tall, and had not even played basketball until he was seventeen years old.

Chapter 2

Dikembe Mutombo grew up in what is now called the Democratic Republic of Congo. From 1971 until 1997, the country was known as Zaire. Mutombo was born in Zaire on June 25, 1966. He was given a very long name: Dikembe Mutombo Mpolondo Mukamba Jean Jacque Wamutombo. In Africa, friends and relatives can each give you a name when they come to see you after you are born. The word *dikembe* means "banana." His father named him that because, as an infant, Dikembe would often fall over to the side, sort of like a banana. "When I was little I was soft. If they sat me up, I fell this way or that way," Mutombo said, laughing.

The Democratic Republic of Congo is a country of about 40 million people, in the center of Africa. The country is about one fourth the size of the United States, with mountains, plateaus, rain forests, and the Congo River Basin. The major crops are coffee, rice, sugar cane, bananas, tea, and mangoes. Also known as a mining country, the Democratic Republic of Congo contains 60 percent of the world's cobalt. Cobalt is used in the making of magnets and is also used to help fight cancer. Copper, gold, and silver are also mined there.

Dikembe grew up in the city of Kinshasa, in a large household that was filled with love and support. He had eight brothers and sisters and also lived with many of his cousins. Sometimes there were up to seventeen people living in the house. Dikembe grew up around a lot of people, and he still likes to surround himself with friends and family.

Education and pride were stressed in Dikembe's house, and all the children were expected to do well in school. His father was the director of the city's high schools. "I came from a stable family," Mutombo said. "I was raised right. Education was the prime priority for us and almost everybody in my family has finished college."

Dikembe was taught that the way around many of the

Growing up, Dikembe's parents stressed that their children have pride and become well educated. Today, Mutombo visits schools to teach children the importance of learning.

problems in this world can be solved through proper communication. He grew up speaking many languages. Today, he speaks English, French, Spanish, Portuguese, and five African languages.

Education was important in Dikembe's house, but athletics was not. When Dikembe was only seven years old, one of his older brothers, Kayinda, died unexpectedly. Kayinda's team had won a championship handball match. He jumped high into the air to celebrate, and then collapsed. The cause of death was never determined, although possibly it was a heart attack. Kayinda was in perfect health, with no history of heart problems. He was also in great shape and was only twenty-four years old.

The incident touched the family deeply, and for a long time, the other children were not allowed to participate in sports. After a while, however, the parents decided that the children could play.

Dikembe was a tall and clumsy child. His parents were tall: His father, Mukamba, was six-feet four-inches tall and his mother, Biamba, was five-feet ten-inches. Dikembe was embarrassed about his height. The other children would often make fun of him. He never wanted to go to the marketplace, because people would stare and laugh. "They thought I was a ghost from another planet, not a kid from the neighborhood," said Mutombo. "It would make me very sad. It was hard for me."

One day, the local newspaper took a picture of the giant Mutombo and put it on the first page. Above Dikembe's picture was a caption that read: "The Giraffe of Kinshasa." This hurt Dikembe a lot. He would remember it forever.

Being tall also caused Dikembe to have some trouble in school. In Africa, it is considered disrespectful for a student to look down at his teachers. But Dikembe could not help it. He was so tall that he had to look down at them. The teachers felt he did not respect them. Life was hard for him.

Dikembe was very close to his family, and he still is. When he was growing up, he would take his blind grandfather for walks nearly every day. Sometimes he would sell bread and jam in the local marketplace, and then share the money he earned with his family and friends.

When he was a child, Dikembe once accompanied his father to a world heavyweight championship fight in Africa. He saw Muhammad Ali fight George Foreman in what was billed as the "rumble in the jungle." Dikembe's father sold refreshments throughout the fight. Dikembe helped his father, but also he was able to watch some of the fight. He liked the power that the fighters seemed to have, how the fans adored them. He wanted to be liked and admired as well.

Mutombo loves to be around people. As a child, he surrounded himself with friends and animals. He had a cat, a dog, and a monkey.

His older brother Ilo, who now works in Washington, D.C., had an explanation for the number of Dikembe's friends. "He loves to be around people, around children," he said. "He loves to talk to people. Much of this is because of my father, who is a beautiful leader and because of my mother, too. It is a matter of ego. Being isolated is not the African way."

Like Hakeem Olajuwon, another African native who became a great NBA basketball player, Dikembe loved to play soccer. In fact, for many years, it was the only sport he played. He developed into a star player during grade school, playing mostly goalie. He played hard and earned a reputation for guarding the net as if his life depended on it. With his tall frame and long arm span, Dikembe was an outstanding goalie.

Dikembe did not play basketball until his senior year in high school. His father told him that because he was so tall, maybe he should try out for the team. But Dikembe was not graceful at all; in fact, he was very clumsy. The first time he

From the time he was young, Dikembe has always surrounded himself with a lot of friends. His brother has said that Dikembe just loves being around people.

ran down a basketball court, he tripped and fell on his face. His brother Ilo was a player for the country's national team, and he helped Dikembe to get better. Soon Dikembe was also on the national team.

Dikembe would read about great NBA players when he passed in front of the United States embassy in Kinshasa. Articles telling about great players were taped to the windows of the embassy.

Dikembe studied hard and decided that he wanted to go to college. Most of Dikembe's family had gone to college: some of them had even traveled as far as the United States to study. Dikembe wanted that, too. One of his sisters lives in Canada, and three of his brothers are in the United States. His cousin Louis Kanda was a surgeon in Washington, D.C., and Dikembe wanted to be near him. He decided to attend Georgetown

University, in Washington, D.C. It was a decision that would change his life forever.

Even though he played basketball during his senior year of high school in Zaire, Mutombo was not serious about sports. In fact, he went to Georgetown on an academic scholarship.

Most people would find it very stressful to move to a country where a different language was spoken. But Mutombo was mature for his age and had a good head on his shoulders. He was also a relatively old freshman at the age of twenty-one. "I came to this country where I knew that I had to be responsible for any action that I take and I had to make sure that I behave myself very well," Mutombo said. "I control myself and every move that I make and I think that's helped take care of me as well."

When he got to Georgetown, Mutombo immersed himself in the English language. He practiced it for seven hours a day for nearly two years.

About a month after he enrolled at the university, several of his friends and classmates came to Mutombo's door. It had snowed, and they wanted him to see what snow was like. Mutombo was annoyed. His friends thought that all Africans were like the ones portrayed in Tarzan movies. They did not know that he had come from a big city and that he had seen snow his entire life on the mountains of eastern Congo. Mutombo made it a point to try to educate his friends about the real Africa.

Until that point, basketball had never been a factor in Mutombo's life. He played it rarely with his friends. One day, while he was working at the university, he was spotted by Georgetown basketball coach John Thompson. The coach was amazed by Mutombo's height and wanted to know if he would try out for the team. "He asked me if I wanted to be part of the team and I picked up the game from there," Mutombo said.

Mutombo's first few times on the basketball court at

In 1987, Mutombo left Kinshasa for the United States. Georgetown University had offered him an academic scholarship.

Georgetown were like a nightmare. He was uncoordinated, and he was far behind the other players on the team in playing skills. Many of his teammates had played basketball most of their lives. To Mutombo, it was still nearly new. There was only one way to get better: hard work. Mutombo decided that he would work as hard as he could to become the best basketball player he could be.

Hard work, like education, was nothing new for him. Growing up he was responsible for many chores around the house and was always expected to work hard. "I took the game into consideration and worked as hard as I could," Mutombo said. "I pushed myself to reach these levels; all it took was a work ethic. I think if you grow up with that work ethic, there's no way you don't get a chance to achieve as you reach an older age."

The hard work paid off, and Georgetown awarded Mutombo an athletic scholarship. The Georgetown Hoyas were a very strong team. Mutombo did not play in his freshman season, but he worked hard and began earning playing time when he was a sophomore. He was not a great scorer, but he established himself as a defensive presence. He was known for not going for offensive fakes and for standing his ground. The Hoyas played in the competitive Big East Conference, which included teams such as Connecticut, St. John's, and Syracuse. As a sophomore, Mutombo showed his promise when he blocked a Big East record 12 shots in a single game.

Coach Thompson began showing more faith in Mutombo and started to put him into some big games. By the time Mutombo was a junior, he and Alonzo Mourning, another future NBA star, were known throughout the college basketball world as defensive terrors. Teams hated to face the two of them; they knew that scoring and rebounding would be very difficult. Beating them would also be hard to do.

Chapter 3

As a junior, Dikembe Mutombo had become a household name in the college basketball world. By the time the season was over, Mutombo and Mourning were named cowinners of the Big East Defensive Player of the Year Award. Mutombo began the year as Mourning's backup. Coach Thompson learned right away that Mutombo could change a game just by being on the court, and he decided to play both players on the floor together. Suddenly, teams that were used to driving the ball at the basket were taking long jump shots instead. Teams that liked to run the ball on fast breaks were suddenly not so eager to tangle it up with Mutombo and Mourning beneath the boards.

By the time Mutombo was a senior, NBA teams were scouting almost every one of his games. It looked as though Mutombo would be drafted into the NBA. Mutombo rose to the challenge of playing in front of scouts every night. As a twenty-five-year-old senior, Mutombo averaged better than 15 points and 12 rebounds per game. He was named the Big East Defensive Player of the Year for the second time.

Awaiting the rebound, Mutombo boxes out an opponent. At Georgetown, it did not take long before Coach John Thompson realized the importance of having Mutombo and teammate Alonzo Mourning together under the basket.

Although he was a big college basketball star, Mutombo did not ignore his studies. In fact, he graduated with a double major, in linguistics and diplomacy.

Mutombo was still not regarded as a great scorer, and by the time the draft approached, it was unclear whether he would go in the first few picks. He hoped to have as successful an NBA career as another Georgetown graduate, Patrick Ewing. He and Ewing became good friends while Mutombo was at Georgetown. They worked together and often practiced basketball all summer long in the Georgetown area.

The Charlotte Hornets had the first pick in the NBA draft, and many people expected them to choose the giant from the Democratic Republic of Congo. After all, they were a talented but undisciplined team that needed a center, a leader, and someone who could play defense. Their two centers were J. R. Reid and Mike Gminski, two players who would be fine reserves elsewhere but who were forced into starting duty for the Hornets. Somewhat surprisingly, Charlotte chose University of Nevada–Las Vegas (UNLV) basketball star Larry Johnson. The Hornets pointed to several raps against Mutombo. They said that he was already too old, at twenty-five, to learn the NBA game. They said that he did not score enough and that at only 240 pounds, he would never be strong enough to hold his own with other NBA centers.

Before the draft, NBA "superscout" Marty Blake was telling teams that a player like Mutombo only comes around every twenty-five years. But not everyone listened.

New Jersey chose next and went for local point guard Kenny Anderson. The Nets needed someone to draw fans away from their popular rivals, the New York Knicks. The Sacramento Kings were third to pick, and it seemed as if Mutombo would end up there. General Manager Jerry Reynolds liked Mutombo a lot. "In Mutombo, you may have one of the top five or six centers in the league in a couple of years," he said.

But Reynolds and Coach Dick Motta disagreed about Mutombo. Motta does not like thin players in the paint, and so he convinced Reynolds to go after Syracuse product Billy Owens. That left the Denver Nuggets up next, with the fourth pick in the draft.

No one expected the high-scoring Nuggets to go after a low-scoring, shot-blocking center. After all, the Nuggets were known throughout the league as an offense-only team. In fact, Coach Paul Westhead had a score-at-all-costs philosophy. The Nuggets did score a lot of points, but they also gave up a lot of points. They allowed 130.8 points per game. They were a terrible team that had lost more than sixty games. Unless Westhead was willing to change his mentality, picking Mutombo made little sense. But that's just what they did.

A few minutes later, the Denver Nuggets proved they were going in a new direction, toward respectability. The Nuggets also had the eighth pick in the draft, and they chose guard Mark Macon, who was also known as a solid defensive player.

For Mutombo, it did not matter what sort of offense his team ran; he was just glad to be in the NBA. And after signing a five-year contract for $13.75 million, he would be able to help out his family and his people back home. "It is an African thing to share your money with your family," Mutombo said. "Besides I don't want to just make money and be happy by myself."

Indeed, over the years Mutombo has helped out his family immensely. He bought a home for his parents, cars for his brothers and sisters, and furniture, and clothes. He even helps out with their mortgages.

His brother Ilo is not surprised at how Dikembe shares his money. "Dikembe has always been [a] generous person, even when he was very little," Ilo said. "If he was eating an orange, he'd always tear off a slice and give it to you."

Nuggets general manager Bernie Bickerstaff was pleased to have a potentially dominating center on his team. But he still had a hard time convincing Coach Paul Westhead to change the strategy of the team. Westhead wanted to go with a wide-open offense, thinking that he could simply outscore the other teams.

That summer, before the season began, Mutombo practiced hard with his friends Mourning and Ewing. They helped him work on his offensive skills. It certainly paid off. Mutombo became more aggressive on the offensive end, although Westhead's offense rarely called for any set plays to be called for his giant center.

In November 1991 he played his heart out. He averaged 19.8 points and 14.7 rebounds in fifteen games. That month, the rookie center beat out everybody else in the NBA when he was named the NBA Schick Player of the Month. The NBA uses a computer formula to calculate a player's impact on his team's success for the month.

It was clear, only one month into the season, that the Nuggets had their best rookie since David Thompson had joined the team in 1975. The team, however, was not much better and on a pace to lose sixty games again. Mutombo was establishing himself as a solid player. Along with guard Chris Jackson, who later renamed himself Mahmoud Abdul-Rauf, Mutombo gave the Nuggets a solid foundation.

While Mutombo was seemingly having an easy time on the court, he was having a harder time in the locker room. He found it hard to communicate with his teammates, because many of the things he wanted to say did not translate well into English.

"You know, there was a time when I didn't really like the

Making a move toward the basket, Mutombo brushes back the defender. Many people were surprised by the amount of offensive skill that he showed during his rookie season.

big guy," said Abdul-Rauf, who became his best friend. "We didn't always communicate well and I wondered about the things he said when he first came here. He'd use the words 'I' and 'me' a lot. But I realize now it's because I didn't really understand him, didn't really understand the way he talked because he came from another country."

Soon it became evident to Abdul-Rauf and the other players what kind of a man Mutombo really was. "I believe now he has a loving heart and really cares about people," Abdul-Rauf said.

Mutombo became known to teammates as someone with a great sense of humor. He would often bellow songs in the shower, and his teammates would all laugh at how terrible his singing voice was. "I guess I won't quit my day job," he would joke back.

Mutombo was the only rookie chosen to play in the 1992 NBA All-Star Game. He scored 4 points as a reserve for the Western team.

At first, Mutombo had some difficulty communicating with his teammates. Once they got to know him, though, they realized that he has a great sense of humor.

Mutombo was on his way to running away with the NBA's Rookie of the Year Award until he tore some ligaments in his left thumb on March 28, 1992. He had to sit out the final two months of the season. He finished the season averaging 16.6 points per game and led the Nuggets with 12.3 rebounds and 2.96 blocks per game. His rebounding average was good enough to rank third in the league. Mutombo finished second to Charlotte's Larry Johnson in the voting for Rookie of the Year. He probably would have won the award if he hadn't been injured.

Dikembe Mutombo had come a long way in a short time, from being mocked for his height to becoming an NBA All-Star. But Mutombo did not stop there. He knew that there was a lot of hard work in front of him.

Chapter 4

Even though Mutombo had such a great rookie season, the Nuggets were still only a few games better than they were the year before. The owners decided to go with a coaching change. It was obvious that the fast-paced, score-at-all-costs offense that Coach Paul Westhead had tried was not working. The Nuggets brought back former Nuggets hero Dan Issel to coach the team. Issel had spent ten seasons playing for the Nuggets and had been elected to the Naismith Memorial Basketball Hall of Fame.

Issel wanted to get the most out of his young players, and he also wanted to begin stressing defense. Although Mutombo was already an outstanding defensive player, Issel felt that he could learn more by working with one of the greatest defensive centers of all time, Bill Russell.

Russell led the Boston Celtics to eleven championships as a player and a coach. During his playing days, Russell was known as the premier defensive player in basketball. Whereas other players wanted the glory of scoring or driving to the basket, Russell was always proud of his defensive skills. He was known for staying flat-footed and spinning around with the shot in midair, then nipping the ball away with his long arms.

Early in his career, Mutombo heard the comparisons to Russell. "I want to be remembered as a guy who could put himself in the same category as Bill Russell," he said.

Mutombo was also getting recognition from other coaches and players in the league. "Dikembe doesn't get the credit he deserves," said NBA player Stacey King, who is a huge Mutombo fan. "A lot of people don't consider shot-blocking to be good defense, they consider it a last resort. But if you've got an intimidator back there . . . it's huge."

Mutombo worked hard with Russell on the subtle things that make a successful defensive player. Russell worked on positioning and footwork, which Mutombo picked up right away. He credited his background in soccer for his ability to move so fast on his feet. Hakeem Olajuwon of the Houston Rockets also credits soccer for his basketball success. Olajuwon has been a great offensive as well as defensive player for many years. He has compared basketball moves with soccer movements many times.

Mutombo took one particular thing to heart, one thing Russell said that would stay with him forever. "It's not so much how many shots you block, Dikembe," Russell told him, "it's how many you challenge."

During his second season, 1992–93, Mutombo once again played solid defense, and this time, under the direction of Coach Issel, the Nuggets showed promise. The team improved to a 36–46 record by getting the most out of the young players. The team could have posted a much better record but fell into a club-record losing streak when they dropped fourteen straight games between December 5 and January 5. Along with Mutombo, there were two other bright spots for the Nuggets. Abdul-Rauf posted career highs in every offensive category

Concentrating on the ball, Dikembe Mutombo rises to block a shot. Mutombo benefited greatly from the advice of Celtics Hall of Famer Bill Russell, considered by many to be the greatest defensive player in NBA history.

and was named the NBA's Most Improved Player. Abdul-Rauf led the team with a 19.2 scoring average. The other bright spot was rookie LaPhonso Ellis, who was named to the NBA All-Rookie first team.

Mutombo averaged 13 rebounds and 3.5 blocks per game. He finished the season with 287 blocked shots. Mutombo also began playing to the fans by waving his finger in an emphatic "no" gesture every time he blocked a shot. Opponents hated it, but the fans loved it.

That season, his scoring average dipped to 13.8 points per game. That did not matter much to the Nuggets. They had the scorers; now they needed the defense. Mutombo grabbed 344 offensive rebounds, second in the league. This meant that Mutombo gave his teammates 344 extra chances to score.

On March 23, 1993, Mutombo pulled down an incredible 23 rebounds against the Miami Heat. Two days later, on March 25, Mutombo produced an unusual triple double. The most common triple double is achieved when a player has ten or more points, rebounds, and assists in a single game. Against the Golden State Warriors that day, Mutombo scored 21 points, grabbed 16 rebounds, and blocked 10 shots. A few weeks later, on April 18, Mutombo scored 16 points, pulled down 21 boards, and swatted away 12 shots. The 12 blocks against the Clippers were the most by any single player in the league for the entire season. He was named NBA Player of the Week for the period ending March 28, 1993.

Dikembe Mutombo is not just on a mission to prove what a great basketball player he is. He is also one of those rare athletes who truly wants to make the world a better place to live in. He does this because he loves people.

He donates a lot of his time and money to causes he feels are worthy. He has given money to build a hospital, he has

Dikembe Mutombo is known for wagging his finger in an emphatic "no" gesture every time he blocks a shot. Opponents hate it, but fans love it.

given money to African Olympic teams, and he has toured poorer parts of his home continent as a goodwill ambassador.

In the summer of 1993, between seasons, Mutombo made big news when he decided to take a goodwill trip to Africa. He had already made the trip twice before with a relief agency called CARE. This time he also went on an NBA-sponsored trip. He brought with him his two closest friends in the world: Patrick Ewing and Alonzo Mourning. They put on basketball clinics in some of the poorest and toughest parts of the world. Mutombo was even able to convince NBA commissioner David Stern to go along.

Mutombo and his friends earned nothing for the trip, which took them to Zambia, Kenya, and Somalia. Because of civil war, Mutombo was unable to return directly to his own country, Congo. It did not bother him much. "Although I am from Zaire [Congo], I consider all of Africa my home and all Africans my people," he said. "On these trips I just try to give hope to people who have no hope. As my father always reminded me, you should remember where you come from, and you should always give something back."

One of the highlights of the trip occurred while the NBA ambassadors were traveling in the slums of Soweto, in South Africa. Many children crowded around Mutombo's van and pleaded to see his gigantic sneakers. The big man smiled and stuck his feet out the window. The crowd roared with delight.

"He's an entertaining young man," said Stern. "I can't say enough nice things about him."

Bill Russell's influence was obvious during the 1993–94 season, as Mutombo led the Nuggets to that improbable come-from-behind victory over the Seattle SuperSonics. So when the 1994–95 season rolled around, basketball experts every-where were expecting Denver to go far in the playoffs, maybe even reach the NBA Finals. That would prove to be difficult.

Mutombo has made many goodwill trips back to Africa. One of the things he does there is hold basketball clinics for children.

Things began to go wrong in the preseason for the Nuggets when their second leading scorer and rebounder, LaPhonso Ellis, tore up his knee during an exhibition game. He was lost for nearly the entire season. Then, early in the season, point guard Robert Pack, who was among the league leaders in assists, injured his knee, too. Then, to make matters worse, just a few weeks into the season, Head Coach Dan Issel became disenchanted with the team. He was burned out. The Nuggets were struggling to keep above .500, with an 18–16 record, when Issel quit. The Nuggets named Assistant Coach Gene Littles as the interim head coach. That experiment did not last long. The team floundered with a 3–13 mark, and Littles was replaced by General Manager Bernie Bickerstaff.

Bickerstaff was the third head coach the team had in just a few months. There was no way this team could rebound and become the power everyone expected it to be. It seemed that Mutombo was the only player who was not affected by the injury bug. He played in all eighty-two games and posted some big defensive numbers. He was even named the NBA Defensive Player of the Year. He averaged 12.5 rebounds and 3.91 blocks per game, as the Nuggets struggled to make the playoffs.

Mutombo led the team in a dramatic win on the final day of the season against the Sacramento Kings for the last playoff spot. The Nuggets finished the season at 41–41, edging out the Kings, who finished 40–42.

The postseason was a disappointment, however, as Denver was swept by the San Antonio Spurs in the first round.

Chapter 5

The summer following the end of the 1994–95 season was a special one for Mutombo. He decided to share more of his wealth and do more for his family than he had ever imagined he could do. In August, Mutombo adopted four children. He adopted the son and daughter of his brother, Kamba, who had died of a brain tumor in 1990. He also adopted the daughter of another brother, Kayinda, who had died after playing handball. Then he adopted the son of one of his sisters, who was unable to care properly for her son.

Mutombo was now a father. He knew that he would have to set a good example for his children. In his first few years in the NBA, Mutombo had earned the reputation of being a player who argued every call made against him. He knew that would have to change.

"Those kids have changed my life," he said. "I feel like I have to grow up and set a good example for them. I want them to see only positive things when they see me on T.V. or when they read about me. I don't want people thinking their daddy's

During 1994–95, Dikembe Mutombo proved that he was of the best defenders in the league. At the end of the season, he received his first NBA Defensive Player of the Year Award.

an idiot and making fun of them. This way, they will be treated with more respect."

Mutombo's newfound attitude translated into his being a calmer player on the court. He tried to stop complaining and be a better sport. The nicer Mutombo did not play less defense. He got even better!

Mutombo firmly established himself as the NBA's most dangerous and best defender. He led the league in blocked shots for the third year in a row. The Nuggets had acquired Antonio McDyess, a strong inside player, from the Los Angeles Clippers. In the 1995 NBA draft, McDyess had been the second player chosen overall. McDyess seemed to be the perfect complement to play alongside Mutombo. But the team still suffered from the absence of LaPhonso Ellis, who missed the first thirty-seven games of the season with that knee injury. The Nuggets started the season with a lowly 1–8 record and never seemed to get on track.

There was another distraction for Mutombo throughout the regular season. His contract was expiring. He wanted a big contract so that he would never have to worry about providing for his four children. He also wanted to be on a team that was committed to winning. He was not sure that the Nuggets were going in the right direction.

Everybody in Denver was hoping that Mutombo would stay with the team. When his neighbors would see him in the street, they would say that they wanted him to remain a Nugget. That touched Mutombo deeply. "Lately they have been telling me that they would miss me too much," he said. "That they would miss my personality. And that feels so nice. It goes straight to my heart."

Speaking of his heart, Mutombo had been lonely for a few years but was now planning to get married. He almost got married in 1994 to a twenty-three-year-old medical student named Michelle. But the wedding was canceled abruptly when Mutombo insisted that she sign a prenuptial agreement. She refused, and the wedding was called off just minutes before it was supposed to happen. Mutombo was criticized in the press, but he firmly believed that he did the right thing.

A few years later, Mutombo met Rose, who is also from Zaire. The couple got engaged while Mutombo was adopting his four children.

Mutombo was unsure what to do about his contract. "I don't know yet, I really don't," he said. "There are days I want to stay and there are days where I'd like to see what I'm worth. I need a lot of money. I'm getting married, I have my kids now, and I have a very big family back home. Man, there's a lot I have to do."

The Nuggets finished with a disappointing 35–47 record and out of the playoff picture. They were, however, one of the handful of teams to defeat the mighty Chicago Bulls. They posted a 105–99 victory over Michael Jordan and the Bulls in Denver on February 4, 1995.

Mutombo established himself further as a great defensive player by leading the NBA in blocked shots for the third year in a row. He also finished third in rebounding and even tied a franchise record on March 26 when he grabbed 31 rebounds against Charlotte. When Mutombo appeared in his third All-Star Game, he scored 4 points and pulled down 9 rebounds in just eleven minutes of play.

When the season ended, Mutombo became a free agent. That meant that his contract had expired and he was now free to play for whatever team he wanted. Of course, not many teams were able to afford him.

The Nuggets management, especially Bickerstaff and team president Tim Leiweke, wanted to keep Mutombo in a Nuggets uniform, but they didn't have enough money.

Leiweke said that he would have to raise ticket prices in order to keep him. Many teams rely on television revenues to help make money and sign good players. Denver is only the eighteenth largest television market in the league.

But something else happened that affected Mutombo's decision as well. On Christmas morning, 1995, he was leaving his house to go to church. Suddenly his doorway was pelted with several eggs. It hurt his feelings deeply. He had always considered the people of Denver to be his friends. "I told myself, they don't want you here," he said.

The Detroit Pistons, Los Angeles Lakers, and Atlanta Hawks were the teams that had expressed the most interest in Mutombo. All three teams were already very good; adding a center would take them to a championship level.

The Hawks, who wanted him most, gave Mutombo the financial security that he had been looking for. In the summer of 1996, Atlanta signed Mutombo to a five-year, $57 million contract. Just a few months before, the Hawks managed to win only one game in the Eastern Conference semifinals against the Orlando Magic. They knew that they needed a defensive presence to help them win.

The team improved immediately once Mutombo became a Hawk. The most obvious improvement, besides team defense, was that talented power forward Christian Laettner was able to move to his natural position. Without a center, Laettner often had to play the center position.

Mutombo and his finger-wag helped the Hawks to win an impressive 56 games and become one of the top defensive teams in the league. They allowed only 89 points per game. No one was happier about the acquisition than Coach Lenny Wilkens.

"Dikembe has been a huge defensive presence for us this season with the job he does in the paint," Wilkens said. "Teams

After the 1996 season, Mutombo signed a free agent contract with the Atlanta Hawks. Mutombo was happy to go to a playoff-caliber team.

can't just walk down the middle on us anymore because Dikembe is there to blocks shots and rebound. He is an intimidating force. Once he has blocked a few shots, guys start looking for him because they know he is there."

Mutombo's defense allowed the Hawks' guards, especially all-star Steve Smith, to gamble more on defense. Smith was able to take chances and go for steals, because he knew that Mutombo was behind him. "Everything we've been able to do has been because of the big fella back there," Smith said.

The fans in Atlanta took to Mutombo right away. They loved his finger-wave. They would imitate him and roar with delight every time he swatted one away. "I just came up with the finger wave and tried to see if it would be accepted," Mutombo said. "Everybody enjoys it, even the fans. Everywhere I go, the fans have signs that say 'No, no no!'"

Mutombo and the Hawks were set to play Grant Hill and the tough Detroit Pistons in the first round of the 1997 NBA playoffs. The Hawks' stifling defense, and Mutombo's dominating play, made for an easy postseason victory. In fact, on April 28, Mutombo showed the league that he could score, not just rebound and block shots.

The Pistons' only true weakness was that they did not have a talented center who could match up against Mutombo, and he took advantage of this. Eagerly calling for the ball, Mutombo scored a career playoff-high 26 points, many of them coming on easy shots, close to the basket. The last two points were punctuated by a tremendous two-handed slam-dunk.

Mutombo was effective in the series despite playing with a very painful strained left groin.

The Hawks advanced to play Michael Jordan and the Chicago Bulls in the Eastern Conference Semifinals. Like everyone else who played in Chicago at that time, the Hawks

The Mutombo-led Hawks squared off against the Chicago Bulls in the second round of the 1997 NBA playoffs. Mutombo averaged over 12 rebounds per game during that postseason.

were mainly concerned with trying to stop Jordan. The plan was to have All-Star Steve Smith play tight on Jordan, and then occasionally use the shot-blocking Mutombo to double-team him.

"He doesn't seem to want to take the ball to the hoop as much," said Hawks coach Lenny Wilkens. "So if we can force him to do something he doesn't want to do, there's one small victory."

The Bulls squeaked out a win in game one, 100–97. But Mutombo took a more active role in the second game. He double-teamed Jordan as often as he could. Near the end of the game, Mutombo jumped out on a Jordan three-point attempt. Although Mutombo missed blocking the ball, he made Jordan alter his shot slightly, forcing him to miss. Now the Hawks had tied the series with a 103–95 win.

Eventually, Jordan and the Bulls proved to be too much for the Hawks to handle. The Bulls won the series, and they went on to win the team's fifth NBA championship.

The Denver Nuggets fell on hard times after Mutombo left. It made him sad to see the arena so empty when he visited in 1998 with the Hawks. There were only 7,525 people in attendance, and some even wore paper bags over their heads in protest.

"It's just sad," Mutombo said. "I remember how this house used to be packed, even if we didn't win."

Chapter 6

Now that Dikembe Mutombo had become a Hawk and had financial security, he really wanted to concentrate on two things. One was winning a championship. The second was helping others.

Mutombo has always been eager to send money back home to Africa for various projects. He also has donated a lot of his time to these projects. Mutombo is always flying back to his home continent and putting on free basketball clinics for children. In Africa, he is regarded as a true hero. Now the dream of building a modern hospital in his home city could be a reality.

One time, when Mutombo was flying to South Africa on a goodwill mission, he was introduced to C. Payne Lucas, who was the president of Africare, a charity group. The two men hit it off and decided to try to work together on a good cause one day. Lucas was very passionate about getting NBA players to help their cause. "I don't care how many NBA millions you have or championships you win. At the end of the day, you have to do something for the world, on the streets of

Mutombo rests his sore knees after a hard-fought contest. No stranger to the field of medicine, Mutombo has worked hard to raise money to build an updated hospital in Kinshasa.

Washington or on the streets of Africa. You have to stand for something," he said.

In the summer of 1998, the two men were reunited at a benefit dinner to help start Mutombo's dream. At that dinner, Mutombo announced that he was donating $2 million to help start his foundation. His goal was to raise nearly $44 million to build a general hospital in his home city.

"It is not an easy mission," Mutombo said. "I must carry the message wherever I go. There are things you must do when you have the opportunity, and becoming a famous athlete in this country gives me the chance to do them."

A few weeks after that dinner, Mutombo flew back to his home city of Kinshasa to check out abandoned buildings or sights for his hospital. There are not many doctors there, and there is a shortage of medical supplies. One in every five children dies before the age of five. Mutombo wants to put an end to all that.

"My greatest hope is to make a difference," Mutombo said. "By building a hospital, maybe we can create something that can last forever."

Other people in Mutombo's family are interested in helping others as well. His uncle, Dr. Louis Kanda, is a cardiovascular surgeon in Washington, D.C. Kanda performs free operations a few times a year in poor countries without good medical facilities. It is a custom in Mutombo's family to help others when you can.

Mutombo's wife, Rose, also realizes that it is his destiny to do good for others. They are raising the four children he adopted. The couple also have a daughter, Carrie, born in 1997. "It is not the law but it is a custom for the one in the family who has been lifted up the most financially to help the children of others," Rose Mutombo said.

Mutombo said that he would be able to die a happy man if

Although he is busy raising money for the hospital, Mutombo still finds the time to talk to young people.

the hospital was built during his lifetime. It is truly his life's work. He really loves children and cares for them.

Edith Sempala, an ambassador from the African country of Uganda, called Mutombo the "Son of all of Africa."

Mutombo continued to dominate on the basketball court as well. He had another great season in 1997–98. He brought his scoring average up to 13.4 points per game, but, more important, he remained a dominating player on defense. He averaged 11.4 rebounds per game and blocked 3.4 shots per game. The NBA does not keep track of the number of shots that were altered by Mutombo. His presence will often make a shooter take a bad shot.

The Atlanta defense was fourth in blocked shots and eighth in points allowed. Mutombo, who was healthy all season, played in every game. It was the fourth time in his career that the durable Mutombo was able to play all eighty-two games.

Dikembe Mutombo also proved that he could score a lot of points when his team needed it. The Atlanta Hawks have a lot of scoring weapons. As a result, Mutombo does not really need to score too often. But, on November 26, 1997, he scored 34 points against the Toronto Raptors. He was also voted the starting center for the Eastern Conference All-Star team. Patrick Ewing, the East's usual starter, was injured, and the fans voted in Mutombo. It was his fifth appearance in the All-Star Game and his fourth in a row. The fans do appreciate good defense. He scored 9 points and grabbed 7 rebounds in the game.

Mutombo was also helping the Hawks to one of the best records in the league and a playoff berth. The Hawks finished with a 50–32 record and were set to face the tough Charlotte Hornets in the first round of the 1998 playoffs.

Many experts figured that the Hawks would take care of

Charlotte and then play a tough series against the defending champions, Michael Jordan and the Bulls.

When the playoffs began, the Hornets really took it to Atlanta. Charlotte beat the Hawks in the first game, 97–87, despite Mutombo's leading all players with 15 rebounds. He dominated the boards again in Game 2 with 9 rebounds, but the Hawks shooters could not hit open shots. The Hornets beat them, 92–85.

For Game 3, Mutombo inspired his teammates with great defense. They dove after every loose ball, they fought for every rebound, and they simply outhustled the Hornets. The Hawks held Charlotte to a measly 64 points, winning, 96–64. Once again, Mutombo led all players with 11 boards. "Defense is something that has come naturally to me," Dikembe said. "But I'm still working to stop not just one player, but a whole team."

During the pregame introductions, Mutombo is already focused on the game.

Despite Mutombo's efforts, Atlanta's season came to an end when Charlotte took game four, 91–82, to advance in the playoffs. Mutombo and his teammates were very disappointed.

After the season, Mutombo was honored with his NBA-record third Defensive Player of the Year Award. While Mutombo was happy to be recognized as the game's greatest defender, and while he loved the big trophy, he would trade it in for a chance at the championship.

The three trophies in four years only made Mutombo even hungrier for a shot at the NBA title. "This is a great honor, not just for me personally, but for my team," Mutombo said. "But as a player, I have a lot to accomplish. In school, I had a thought that I could reach this level. But hopefully, one day I'll see myself in a championship. This is wonderful, but there's one thing holding me up. I want to play in a championship and win."

It is that attitude and desire that have made Mutombo a favorite in Atlanta among the fans and the coaching staff. "Deek [Dikembe] has all the knowledge in his head and he wants to go out there every night and use all the moves and play a complete game," said Atlanta head coach Lenny Wilkens. "We can see great progress in the two years he's been with us. But sometimes, when he's out there in the heat of a game, it's not that simple. . . . He pushes his energy production up to another level defensively, and I really believe defense influences games. You certainly have to score points, but if you don't have that presence defensively, you could be in for a long night."

Wilkens should know what he is talking about. The coach is the only person ever to be inducted into the Naismith Memorial Basketball Hall of Fame twice! He was inducted after a brilliant playing career, and later for being the winningest coach of all time.

Flying through the air, Dikembe Mutombo is about to throw down a slam dunk. Mutombo's main job is defense, but he has been known to score when his team needs it.

The Hawks had big plans, but unfortunately, for them and for all the NBA teams, the 1998–99 season was delayed. The teams' owners locked the players out during the summer over a contract dispute. The season did not begin until the first week of February 1999.

While Mutombo was active in the union's efforts to reach an agreement with the owners, he was also very involved in his other two loves: raising his family, and raising money to build his hospital in Africa.

Mutombo's dream of building a hospital may soon become a reality. The government of his country has recently changed. The new leaders have expressed an interest in working with Mutombo. They have even told Mutombo that they might be able to provide him with the land for the hospital. "The new government provides a new opportunity," he said.

The owners and players eventually settled the lockout, and planned a shortened schedule of 50 games in about eighty days. A veteran team such as the Hawks would benefit from this. They had a solid nucleus of players that had been together for several years.

Mutombo's stellar defense and Steve Smith's sharp shooting led the Hawks to a 31–19 record and a playoff berth. Mutombo, himself, had another fine season. He led the league in total number of rebounds (610). He was also fourth in the league in blocked shots (147). After the season he won the 1999 IBM Award, given to the player who makes the greatest overall contribution to his team.

There would be a new champion this year. Michael Jordan had retired prior to the start of the season and the Bulls traded away Scottie Pippen. The defending champs did not even make the playoffs. Mutombo and the Hawks had as good a chance as any team to be the next champs.

The Hawks started the playoffs strong by quickly disposing

of Grant Hill and the Detroit Pistons. Unfortunately for the Hawks, they ran into the hottest team in the Eastern Conference in the second round.

The New York Knicks used their quickness and athleticism to sweep the Hawks in four games. The Knicks went on to defeat the Indiana Pacers for the Eastern Conference crown.

After failing to make the playoffs the following year, the Hawks faced a dilemma in 2001. Mutombo was in the final year of his contract and they were concerned he would sign with another team after the season. So rather then let him leave, they traded him to the Philadelphia 76ers for Theo Ratliff and Toni Kukoc. Philadelphia had the best record in the Eastern Conference at the time of the trade.

"I'm going to Philadelphia to play with a great player, Allen Iverson, a scoring machine who plays with tremendous energy," Mutombo said. "The opportunity to win a championship is certainly there."

Sixers fans know that their chances of winning that championship are certainly improved with Mutombo in town.

Career Statistics

College

YEAR	TEAM	GP	FG%	REB	AST	PTS	AVG
1988–89	Georgetown	33	.707	109	5	129	3.9
1989–90	Georgetown	31	.709	325	18	331	10.7
1990–91	Georgetown	32	.586	389	52	487	15.2
Totals		96	.644	823	75	947	9.9

NBA

YEAR	TEAM	GP	FG%	REB	AST	STL	BLK	PTS	AVG
1991–92	Denver	71	.493	870	156	43	210	1,177	16.6
1992–93	Denver	82	.510	1,070	147	43	287	1,131	13.8
1993–94	Denver	82	.569	971	127	59	*336*	986	12.0
1994–95	Denver	82	.556	*1,029*	113	40	*321*	946	11.5
1995–96	Denver	74	.499	871	108	38	*332*	814	11.0
1996–97	Atlanta	80	.527	*929*	110	49	*264*	1,066	13.3
1997–98	Atlanta	82	.526	932	82	34	*277*	1,101	13.4
1998–99	Atlanta	50	.512	*610*	57	16	147	541	10.8
1999–00	Atlanta	82	.562	1,157	105	27	269	942	11.5
Totals		685	.528	8,439	1,005	349	2,443	8,704	12.7

GP=Games Played **FG%**=Field Goal Percentage **REB**=Rebounds
AST=Assists **STL**=Steals **BLK**=Blocks
PTS=Points **AVG**=Points Per Game *Italics*=League Leader

Where to Write Dikembe Mutombo:

Mr. Dikembe Mutombo
c/o Philadelphia 76ers
3601 S. Broad Street
Philadelphia, PA 19148

On the Internet at:

http://www.nba.com/playerfile/dikembe_mutombo.html
http://www.nba.com/sixers/index.html?nav=page

Index